WORDS EXPRESSING FEELINGS

VIMALA THANGGAVILO

Contents

Contents

Contents

Preface

We humans express our feelings by words at an emotional level to others. Free to say but limit it for self-benefit as not everything we express will be visible to everyone. Words could hurt or give joy to ourselves and the people surrounding us. Use wisely as the word has the power to build and destruct. Let it benefit oneself and others in this journey. Words are found in many languages to express oneself respective feelings.

Words Expressing Feelings catered beautiful words and a buffet treat for the readers. Conjointly penned by beautiful co-authors in conjunction with individual preference to express their thought and feelings through words. Thank you for everyone's efforts to make it happen.

Preface

We humans express our feelings by words as an emotional [illegible] free to say but limit it for self-benefit as not everything we express will be [illegible] to everyone. Words could hurt or give joy to others [illegible] a [illegible] as the word has the power [illegible] one [illegible] and others in this journey. [illegible] to express oneself [illegible]

[illegible] feelings cannot be [illegible] words [illegible] beautiful [illegible] express their thoughts and feelings [illegible] thanks to [illegible] everyone's efforts [illegible] happen.

1. Vimala Thanggavilo

T. Vimala is the youngest daughter of Mr. & Mrs. S.Thanggavilo M.Thevanai. She was born and lives in Malaysia. Written more than 200 quotes and poems. Instagram @fun_luv_joy and @uninterruptible_quotes. Co-Author for over 30 anthologies. We are grateful for everyone's support. Thank you.

Life Phrases

Mingle with thoughts,

Before uttering the words.

Befriend with emotion,

Get synchronized before reacting.

Choose the question and answer,

Grateful ever instead regretful forever.

Praise yourself for good deeds,

And warn of any mistake or fault.

If no guilty feelings,

No assurance of saving integrity and credibility.

Credentials of oneself projected with proof in every action,

Not based on self-interest matters.

One should be able to analyze deeply,

To ensure that it suits oneself.

Power is to monitor own self,

Powerless to someone for their genuine act.

Appraisal of self,

Be done truthfully to own self.

Skills to generate success,

Not by intentionally failing others.

2. Meracil S. Horca

Meracil S. horca

Date of birth: october 17 1994

She learn how to write a poem when she was 23 years old. Her teacher told them to create a poem, that was 4 years ago and since then, she loved to write poems to express her emotion to say what she feel and make it as an art. She is from Philippines.

2. [illegible]

[illegible]

Date of birth: [illegible]

[illegible] teacher told them [illegible] poem, [illegible] [illegible] she [illegible] to [illegible] to say what she feel and wrote it as an art. She is from Philippine.

Broken By Meracil

A broken piece of me.

Cries silently.

To kept the pain on my own only.

It's hard to pretend that I'm ok.

But deep inside of me

Was bleeding thoroughly.

For this heart of mine.

No one can define.

The suffering that lies deeply.

I know someday it will heal.

But the fragments will still remains.

And will never be forgotten.

3. Mukami Kinyua

Mukami Kinyua , currently studying Analytical Chemistry, 22 years of age, Kenyan

THOUGHT I WAS

Thought I was a poet

Who could read through the waves and thoughts of people

To fail I have done them

Thought I was a rainbow poet

Could fly across the sky

Create peace of mind

Essence of love

But have failed what I thought I was

Now I sit alone, lonely

Reflecting on the nightmares beheld

Trying find a solution

With the hope that million dreams will happen

The stars shall light up

And I will be the poet

I thought I was.

4. Churchil Odhiambo Orowe

Churchil Odhiambo Orowe is born and raised in Nairobi Kenya. He is an author, script, and poem writer. His motivation was never to die spiritually but to inspire mentally.

He kept writing many poems to motivate and inspire others through his knowledge.

IG ID which is churchil_painkiller

MY WORK THEY HATE

In the middle of the street my pen complains

Am deeply swimming in the ocean of hate

Indeed in this field of art enemies I create

I won't be wrong to open that shame I get

With open heart I swear

That's the street is full of blood

My pen totally bleeding

And here lonely I do regret for joining poetry

Sometimes in the lonely room I cry

My chic has turn to be pool of tears

Can't check my social media handles

For criticism all they comment at my work

Wish I would turn back the clock

For me to rewrite my wrongs

My mistakes now the price I do pay

And people's statement hurts more than sward.

5. Kipkorir Amos

Kipkorir Amos is a 19 year old poet who ventured in the world of writing while in Highschool, form 3. The first year student of English and literature from Kaimosi Friends University College is also a novelists short story writer and also script writer. A Walk Before Darkness is among anthologies Kipkorir took part. You can reach him through +254700209500/+254700144013

LET US END

My sunshine, where are you?

I know I made repulsive mistakes,

That drew us apart,

I have known your value.

Like fish, you were,

Forward ever,

Coming back is a miracle,

If so,allow it today.

Like butterflies, I'm,

Flying knowing I have few days remaining,

You were my everything,

Addicted to your love,

Nowadays roses aren't red,

With a pleasant aroma and fragrance,

It's black,

Love isn't love without you.

I'm under pain because of you,

I know you're under pain because of me,

Look! We are now even,

Let us end this.

Like movie, our marriage was,

We've now reached the climax,

Let falling resolution starts,

And we'll steer a new life.

Allow an ending dear,

Let us move out of bitter love,

To a sweet like vanilla,

I'm at the door waiting for you.

6. Julián Alberto Guillén López

My name is Julián Alberto Guillén López, I was born on May 8, 1998. In the city of Minatitlán, Veracruz. I'm proudly Mexican. As a poet I started from the age of 12, having conquered several places in Orthography, in addition to a third and second place in a regional contest. I am currently working on my first book of poetry entitled Cornucopia.

Where I take a tour of the different stages of poetry.

In addition to periodically publishing my poems in different magazines and newspapers around the world.

Often

Often

You steal from me

The expressions

When they threaten

Out of my mouth.

You know I have to say

And you drive me

As a professional thief.

The goldsmith recognizes

Your finesse

Just by taking a look at you,

You're full of art.

You give me terrible blows to the ego.

If I don't find you,

I'm going to get you.

What the fuck do I intend

By encysting

In front

To the last of your body?

I Love You

And I know that,

Because not easy

Assimilating soil

The beauty

Of an illusion.

But because of the noise, hubbub

That drives my mouth.

I ask God to be the water

Of your lagoons,

For today, for yesterday and forever.

To assert me from your hips.

Live connected to your essence.

I'm staying overnight

And my prayers

They end up in security

Of your incense.

Your incense.

Inciting to dance for the prose of the Trent.

Futilely looking for someone who can flatter you

And sign the poem under my name.

I feel unworthy but I am writing to you because I love you as an emblem.

Because I want you in my scene.

Julián Alberto Guillén López

Date: 23/03/22

Country: Mexico

7. Rangeesh Chandrasekar

Rangeesh Chandrasekar is a MBA Finance and Marketing graduate staying at Chennai. He is passionate about writing and a great lover of books and articles who has Co authored in 800+ anthologies and compiled over 8+ anthologies.

Why not a girl

Every girl has Maa Durga inside her, just open that invisible third eye Trinayan of consciousness of education and be the durga to kill all the evil minds by the weapon of your wisdom and sharp words.

People Pray For A Boy Not Of A Girl. They Desire A Boy Not Of A Girl. They Love To Have A Boy Not A Girl. Blessings Of Elders Are For Male Not For Female. But In Need Of Wealth They Worship Goddess Lakshmi, In Need Of Education They Worship Goddess Saraswati, In Need Of Courage They Worship Goddess Durga,

Now Tell Me,

Why Do They Hesitate To Have A Devi In Their Family?

8. Maryum Sultan

Maryum is a poetess and a writer. Starting her journey of words, she has painted some dreams. She has participated in many anthologies. Her ambition is to write the mixture of emotions and realities on the paper of reader's hearts. She gathered her dreams of being a language for the unsaid thoughts and emotions and to achieve her aim, she has chosen to write words.

Feelings unanswered

I put my question on the table to be answered,

But there was a silence.

The feelings once they appreciated now are left .

. They are standing at the little distance watching my feelings crying,

Craving for response, but they left them untouched, unheard, unanswered.

Like the waves in the ocean those never reach to the shore, die in between

the journey to the destination.

9. Sandra Bempong

Am An African, A Ghanaian, A Passionate Writer And I Want To Go Places And Impact. Am A Student As Well But Now Impacting Lives Through My Writing.

The One

How can I say this.

My mouth can't open.

It remains shut.

Hmm dreams continue to nag me.

I don't know why,

I still think about you.

Maybe it's an illusion.

I know you don't know.

But I want you to know how I feel.

Your name remains in the hidden part of my memory.

Even if I get amnesia,my love for you won't cease.

If Ever I find You.

I will explain to You.

I close my eyes,

I see you.

My heart melt like ice.

Send me to the perfect place.

Where I will welcome you with an embrace.

A perfect life without you is death.I can go outside time to find you.

I'm obsessed with you.

I can die and reincarnate.

I can't wait for your touch.

Your hot body on mine.

Our sweats together and we bonding in love ?.

10. Binod Dawadi

He is Binod Dawadi from Purano Naikap 13, Kathmandu, Nepal. He has completed his Master's Degree from Tribhuvan University in Major English. He likes to read and write literary forms. He has created many poems and stories. His hobbies are reading, writing, singing, watching movies, traveling, gardening, etc.

He likes pets. He is a creative man he does not spends his time by doing nothing. He is always helping for the poor people. He can't see the troubles and obstacles of the people. He believes that from the writing and from the art it is possible to change the knowledge and perspectives of the people towards any things. He loves his country Nepal very much. He has known many cultures of his country as well as foreign countries. He is always thinking wisely towards any things. He solves his problems by using his mind. He dreams to be a great man in his life.

Mail : vinoddawadi9@gmail.com

What's APP : 9779860513496

Feelings Towards Poor

I can't see their,

Troubles I can't saw,

Them sleeping,

In the road,

I can't see their dirty clothes,

Their life,

Rear in the dirt's,

Who will loves to you ?

I am also poor so,

I can't help them,

But I have very,

Good feelings towards,

The other,

The helpless poor people.

Good feelings rewards

He helps poor people

11. Amb. Maid Corbic

Maid Corbic from Tuzla, 22 years old. In his spare time he writes poetry that repeatedly praised as well as rewarded. He also selflessly helps others around him, and he is moderator of the World Literature Forum WLFPH (World Literature Forum Peace and Humanity) for humanity and peace in the world in Bhutan. He is also the editor of the First Virtual Art portal led by Dijana Uherek Stevanovic, and the selector of the competition at a page of the same name that aims to bring together all poets around the world. Many works have also been published in

anthologies.

A FAITH THAT CONNECTS EVERYTHING

In life we need to love all the people around us

I know that my behavior is very important

Both for me and for my children who will absorb everything

And faith is the best indicator of all stages of life

In general, Christianity is a wonderful faith that exists

Because since childhood I have converted to this faith

Primary Islam; but I believe that every faith teaches

To be better people – and I've always been that way

I help the people around me as selflessly as I can

I know that my destiny is what I create

Christianity has various customs that must be respected

How happy nature would be and our living spirit itself

I find that all faiths are very wonderful and encourage me

To be a good man and spread love to everyone

But if someone asked me, I would choose Christianity

Because there's something in it that drives me every day

The Bible is one of them that I read every day

I can never get bored of her, because in the book

There is much that can be learned and understood

That the world is the way I actually create it

Time is just a general optical illusion that exists

The Spirit lives in me with perseverance that faith lives

The best protection from all troubles is only love

Which I always give unselfishly to everyone around me

Christianity is a faith that, like others, encourages

To spread love and humanitarianism to the world constantly

Because everything I create is only for this life

Yet everything passes and comes quickly, but love one does not!

12. Keabetswe S Lelaka

Keabetswe Lelaka is a very passionate person about writing, his journey began at school at a very young age. He has been in many arts activities including Stage comedies. He believes a pen and paper is a biggest microphone that reaches all angles of the universe.

LIES

I feel distant to the world,

I got a story to tell but don't know where to begin,

I've cost many eyes to lose their tears,

I've lost trust of many hearts,

I have sabotaged a lot.

Lies, you were so sweet,

You got me overcoming anything,

Coming out smoothly from my mouth,

But setting traps along the way as you were taking me higher.

Deserted me when I had to recall you,

Dumped me in a big hole of trash and ran away.

Got caught and punished.

Till I went back to the truth with my head faced down.

I lost my dignity, my respect and my family.

I damaged so many things and I'm incapable of fixing any.

I scammed the innocent and robbed the poor,

Now I'm left with shame and regrets.

Ooh lies, you destroyed my life,

Made me feel like a king for a while,

And disappeared when karma was approaching.

With all my heart, I hate you lies.

13. Ritu Gupta

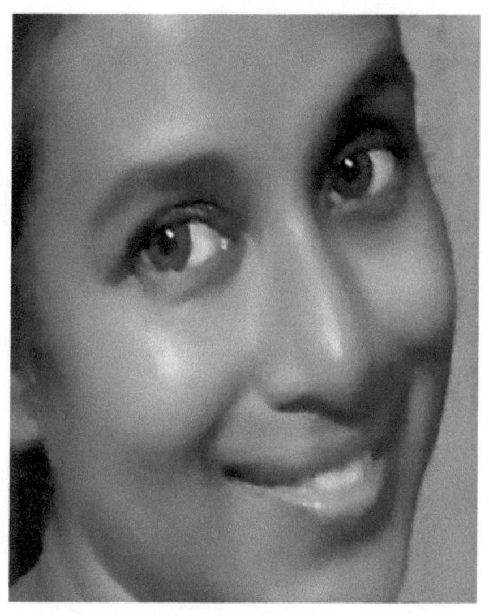

Ritu@Ritz, A Simple Person with a thousand dreams in her heart. A Survivor since the start, she faces the storms that are sent to tear her down. A teacher and a Counselor by profession with a motto to serve the World, she has bagged many prizes and recognitions in the field of Education, Art, Photography, Music and Social Work. She has a passion for travelling and dancing. Loves cooking and is a Crazy Brat but doing harm to none. Believes In Spreading Smiles And Positivity Around!

Her Mantra is,

"You May See Me Struggle,

But You Will Never See Me QUIT!"

SILENCE" IS NOT EMPTY, IT'S FULL OF ANSWERS -ONLY IF YOU CAN HEAR IT…

If you ever feel that people become silent only when they are wrong, you may be wrong to think that.

The difference in opinion can cause disagreement even between two people who are deeply in love with each other. When these disagreements aggravate, they can become harsh exchange of words.

Most of the times, people exchange harsh words not because they truly mean it but they want to win the agreement. They might become loud and even scream out of frustration and rage. The idea is actually to prove them right or better over the other person. Not everyone likes to resolve their issues with noise. Some people choose silence because more than the disagreement, what hurts them is the noise. Their silence is often mistaken as their weakness, wrongdoing or acceptance of mistake. The reality is that these people are the ones who want to save their relationship from pain by keeping their pain in their heart by remaining silent.

Never try to suppress someone just because they are silent. Being silent is not about being wrong. It is about respecting other person's opinion so that both can move on.

14. Fortunate Varaidzo Gwandu

She's a fourth year medical student at Midlands State University Gweru Zimbabwe. She's a 23 year old self motivated writer and poet. She involves herself in leadership roles in and outside of school with issues concerning student advocacy and women empowerment. She has managed to write for Safrap newsletters Swaziland thrice since 2020. Has led Zimbabwe Medical students association at university level from

2020-2021. Aspiring to become a paediatric specialist and a writer.

Pulse!

That knacking sound that resembles the heart beat

The heart being myogenic beats on its own

But mine only beat in his eyes

I depended on his soul to breathe

To be able to make it through a day

In his presence I slept soundly

Like a bluetooth radar, my heart reached null beating

When he went away

I realised I needed his air to breathe

My heart itself was weak

I was too far on the heart donor list

I could only live by him

As I stared in the snow fields

The ripper took his life and I couldn't watch

My heart quit bit by bit

I blinked my last as I lost my life

Then I knew, he was my heart

How I hoped to ressurect with my heart

How I hoped the statement ‘Souls reunite’

Would be true for us

For in my next life I still couldn’t love anyone else

15. Sabita Dakua

Sabita Dakua resides at Mumbai, Maharashtra and has completed masters in business administration. She is persuing her psychology studies as well as compiled 2books, 1Solo and participated in 15+ books as co-author. She is highly motivated with many multi skills and still seeking knowledge to groom self. In her free time she likes to visit new new places, designer and also foodie.

Distance love

Fights and jealousy was at peak,

Again started a new freak,

Let's just chase our own soul break,

Before any emotions outbreak.

Love you my lovely partner,

You are my soul designer,

Practice becomes perfect retainer,

My feelings overwhelms when you are gardener.

Emotions attached feelings with us,

I am always fear and nervous,

Almighty God please bless make courageous,

Relations always stay alive as plus.

-©words_clubbed_

16. Sushmaa Subramanian

Sushmaa Subramanian grew up in the city
Famous for Stainless steel, Magnesite,
Handloom textiles and Mettur dam, with
Big dreams. Travelling, reading novels are
Her favorite hobbies. Reading is what
Makes her feel alive. She aspires to start a
Charitable trust that would support and
Educate special children. She's a compiler of 4 anthologies. She's a
published co-author of 100+anthologies.
To share your

Feedback and for more information, Contact her at-

Email- sushmaa.trs@gmail.com.

Instagram- Sush_twinkle_07

Unemployment

Kavin is from a lower middle class. His parents earn their income from daily wages. All his friends come from different ranks in societies. Kavin topped SSLC exams in his school and state topper also. He got free admission in the same school and continued his higher secondary education and topped his school again and got state second. He joined an arts and science college. His parents became sick as they're getting old. He applied for nearly 1000 jobs. Wherever he approached, he's sent back with a negative response.They rejected him that he's over qualified and some said that he's not qualified for this job and few told him that they prefer experienced persons.He's desperately in need of job to support his family and to take care of his sick parents. He didn't get any job. His parents health deteriorated. He didn't stop. He tried 2000 more jobs. Still, he received the same responses in different terms. Days and years passed by. Kavin continued his job hunt.One morning Kavin's parents found Kavin applying for jobs and making calls. They couldn't control their tears. Their tears came down because Kavin was not making the calls and applying for jobs really. He had gone crazy. He lost his mind. He was too focused in finding a job. The stress of unemployment filled his mind completely and he lost himself. From then, whenever Kavin sees anyone in the street, he asks them for a job. Even today, he's asking for jobs but chained to a wall.

17. Zahra

Zahra is a teenager. She loves to read and write books. She has Participated in many anthologies . She loves to write motivational Words for other people. She loves write her thoughts and share It with others. She loves to write her thoughts and share It with others.

Sharing

I am a teenager,life has taught me a lot of lessons and I want to share some of them..

-nowadays desire of dying is more than desire of trying

-There is a big difference between being selfish and being selfmate

-Everyone who knows your story can understand your pain but no one can feel it

-many people suffer in silence not because they want it because they know that no one cares

-let your anger be this expensive that no one can have it and let your smile this cheap that the poorest person can also have it

-the one who forgives is greater than the one who apologizes

-you are born alone and you have to die alone

18. Macbeth Mwalim Banda

I was born on 20th March, 1994. I have done my Bachelor's Degree of Accountancy at Catholic University in Blantyre, Malawi. I have written a number of books, Novels and authors over 150 poems.

CAGED BEHIND BARS

Sorrowful and gloomy this hole you call home is,

Fruitless punches we throw are blown in vain

Though I've been cornered my whole life,

But I never quite to break these shackles of strife

No light we see, no fresh air we inhale these days,

Only dank air performed with the stench of the prisoners

How long shall we remain in these leg irons?

And when shall we get rid of these heartless morons?

From this cracky wall is where our hope lays,

Hoping to be free and live a life to the fleet

A life which will bring enjoyment like paradise,

When all the grief and pain are buried like clothes in a hatcheck

19. Wafi Fadhlurrahman

Wafi Fadhlurrahman from Indonesia is a writer. He is a 6th semester student from Cirebon City, Indonesia majoring in communication science. He is interested in writing and has written several times for organizations on campus.

Mother : Angel Without Wings

Mom…..

I wrote this poem for you

Strong woman who has been pregnant me for 9 months

A great woman who has taken care of me from the time I was born until now

Mom……

I know you always slip my name in your every pray

I know you always cry thinking about me

Mom……

Tirelessly you serve us

With all the pride in my heart

It doesn't occur to me for a moment to think about your tiredness

You keep walking among the thorns

Mom…..

I don't know how to repay all your services

Even this whole world will never be enough to replace your kindness

Mom…..

You are my angel

I pray that you are always happy

20. Vedika verma

Vedika is a 19 year old gal , pursuing BBA UG degree from PPN College . She is a rookie in this industry but loves to expand her wings and explore the world of possibilities . She has been writing since years but has got the opportunity to prove that she's not less than anybody when it comes to expressing your feelings through pen . She has had several accolades in academics and now wants to know much more about this "forthcoming encounter of her new discovered skills ." She has been the co author in more than 20 anthologies. She is a compiler of 2 anthologies. She regularly participates in the weekly quiz of BAP publications and has been winner there.

BELIEVE YOU CAN

The string that bridges the gap between two persons and builds a brawny companionship is BELIEVE .

The fortitude that enables a preggy to endure nine month's agony is her BELIEVE that one day she would sing lullaby for her baby.

The vigour that aids a gal to bear up apartness from her beloved with a sonrisa is her BELIEVE that one day she would hear his smile.

The inner spirit that provides a determination to a mountaineer to clamber the Everest is her BELIEVE that one day she would hoist her nation's flag at the Everest's peak.

Discrepancy that lies between an achiever and a non-achiever is BELIEVE.

Your BELIEVE that you can motivates you to act and only by acting in appropriate manner, you can clinch your ends.

So, I conclude by pleading you to just BELIEVE

YOU CAN AND YOU'RE ALREADY HALFWAY THERE.

Penned by:-

V...Ved

21. Margaret wairimu waweru

Margaret wairimu is a twenty five year old Kenyan citizen who is passionate about poetry and mental health. She is finishing her master's in literature in a local Kenyan university.

AFRICAN WOMAN

I am not a girl ,

I am just too bold,

Trying to get through as a woman,

In a period where women are LESS HUMAN

I wake up when the spirits are still roaming the earth

I walk to my stall least my family sleeps hungry

I shout day long to attract my customers

I do more than a normal human can

Or how else would I survive in Africa ?

I am not just an African woman

Or how would you explain the savings in my bank account ?

How would you explain the independence I possess ?

All alone with no help of a man

I pay more tax than my earnings

I work more hours than I rest

I fight for the air I breath

I struggle to keep my breath

I get strong for myself when I feel weak

I have hardened my heart like my skin color

I have readied myself to make heaven out of Africa.

I Am not just a woman

I Am a super being

With power bestowed to me from the gods

I am a super natural

I am an African woman

©magi

Words from my soul

22. John Mohamed Mosere

John Mohamed Mosere is a Sierra Leonean, Poet, Writer, Motivational speaker. He is a Catholic Christian. In Poetry world, he goes by the name, "MOSERE D'POET".

He was born in BO Town, at the Bo government hospital in BO district, Southern region, Sierra Leone. He had his nursery and early primary education done at his hometown. Where he wrote to the National Primary School Education(N. P. S. E.)

BRIDGE

Is it not a bridge?

It is a bridge. The longest—So they say

In the whole country. When not a bridge

You'll find a print of groundnuts

Stacked like pyramids,

Or palm trees,or cocoa-trees,and farmers.

Hacking pods, and workmen

Felling trees and trying skinned logs

Into rafts. A thousand letters

By road,by rail,by air

From one end of the world to another

And not one head of beauty on the stamp?

But I once saw John letter with a head of bronzing.

PØËT: JØHŃ M MØSËRË

23. Reena Upadhyay

Reena Upadhyay ,a girl resident of bilaspur chhattisgarh believes " a drop of ink can make a million think". She's currently in 12th and pursuing commerce . Writing and reading something gives her bliss. She's interested in literature especially in poetry.she writes in Hindi and also English. Other than writing she's fond of food. She wants to travel the world and taste every cuisine in future while continuing with the passion of writing

I think

I think stars are kind.

As they radiate light for us

To find solace in this misery of our life

Even though they don't have of their own

Billions and billions of stars in the airspace

Sparkling the night with some glitter of grace

Giving the spectator hopes in their eyes

As they fall to let other's wish

And as the time flies ,sun rises

Falling star has filled the soul with joy and bliss

24. Natasha Moyo

Natasha Moyo is 23 year old student studying at the National University of Science and Technology. Bulawayo resident. Poet and short story writer.

LOVE: THE IDEA

Love. They say it's a beautiful thing. Fairytales talk about happily ever after and the power of true love. Snow white broke the evil Queen's curse with a true love's kiss. Granted it was from a man she barely knew, but we overlook that part. It sort of creates this narrative that women are the damsel in distress and men are their saviors.

Love is truly beautiful when you think about it, write about it or idealize it. But how come love is only targeted towards women. Through fairytales that we as young women read from an early age, we are sort of brainwashed into aspiring to be in love, while boys play video games where they are rescuing princesses from towers and evil sorcerer. In action movies, the hero always has to save some tall, lean, beautiful blond women (the woman changes in almost every James Bond movie by the way, Is that a testament to the fact that men can't commit to one woman or shouldn't? Through what we consume through the media we have been given a warped sense of what love is. Apparently love is about waiting for a prince and saving a damsel in distress.

In this short write up, I challenge you to change your views about love, unlearn the toxic idealization and see it for what it truly is; the emotional connection that only lovers can share, the unbreakable bond. That's love.

25. Jyotsna k

Jyotsna, is a 21 year old girl from chennai city if Tamilnadu. She is an artist by passion and engineer by profession. She is a budding writer, coauthored few anthologies and she is the compiler of the anthology entitled "The Chronicles of Selflove"

Quotes

Quote 1

Fate

Dare to accept

Difficult to forget

Challenging to reinvent

Quote 2

sleepless nights with my pillow

When I am happy

It becomes my teddy

When I burst into tears

It becomes my tear graspers.

Quote 3

The happiness in sleepless nights…

The sorrowness in tearful nights…

Gifted by him

Is irreplaceable…

Quote 4

Late nights…

Perfect buffer zone where the battle between thoughts takes place,

Quit not far as you are still in war.

26. Katie Lauren Thomas

Originating from a small English town, known as Rotherham, writing has always been a great passion of Katie Lauren's. Writing is an open and expressive way of conveying emotion, and is an amazing way to escape current reality. She hopes to someday openly showcase her work, at the hopes of inspiring others with her work.

Feeling inspired

Feeling dull and uninspired

Tried to sleep, but feel too tired

Drifting off to find some space

Walls that reek of doom and gloom

Feeling trapped inside a tomb

It suddenly changed when I saw your face

No words, just a look

And I'm feeling inspired

I looked at you

Then looked away

Unsure of what is right to say

I played along with all the games

The basic small talk at the start

It then devolved into music and art

I finally think I found my way

No need for signals, just a look

And I'm feeling inspired

The dream is perfect

I'll never let you go

Even if it proves to be untrue

Don't ever wake me up

I'll spend my life in my head

I'll dream my life away

As long as it makes you stay

A thought that sticks inside my mind

Is having wisdom a waste of time?

It's all I think 'till I can't sleep

My brain it tells me to give up

There is no pay in what you love

But your spirit came through for me

No need for words, just a look

And I'm feeling inspired

Please don't let the stars at night burn out

Please don't let the morning sun shine through

Please don't let the stars at night burn out

Please don't let the morning sun shine through

27. Sameeha

A 19 year old girl with dreams of becoming an author one day holding a pen she started her journey in the year 2017. Her inspiration is her father who motivates her to read and write more. He was his own writer. His funny- meaningful poetries were
The start.

LOVE

This word always make me wonder and leave me with unanswered questions.

What really is love? How is it? What does is feel like? What are the other shapes of love? Why do the little heart ♥ mean love? Why do some people say that 'love is in the air'? Is it atmosphere?

So much so much to ask!

But I was always left with no answer in the end.

So I decided I will define what I feel is love!

It is everything!

There is love in the hate!

There is love in the pain!

There is love in the heart break!

There is love in the way you breathe!

There is love in the way you smile! Or just your smile is love!

There is love in your sister/brother!

There is love every where!

To see that you have to open your hear

28. Ryan Zibani

Ryan Zibani is from Zimbabwe like to write poetry since age of 17
Studied in Zimbabwe (final year in highschool)

I feel everything !

The people,

The gravity,

The vibration of the earth's rotation,

The heat coming out of my body,

The blood running through my veins,

The deepest thoughts in my mind, that silenced my inner peace.

The coldness of my heart being haunted by my past.

The characters of different personalities in me,

Personalities that weakend my body as it aims to control my soul.

The brutality of my emotions to the nature of my existence in this world,

I feel it all.

29. Joyce Namirembe

Joyce Namirembe,22 years old.
She's a Ugandan but currently living in Kenya.
She's a writer, graphic designer and a mobile photographer.
Been a co-author in more than 245 anthologies.

Started writing at the age of 14.

**Insta id:* joyce_namirembe*

Every time you come close

Every time you come close,

I want to award you with a rose.

Your lips are like silk

Your skin is like milk Those

These eyes are an ocean

And you fill me up with emotions

Hold a little tighter

To keep me ignited like a lighter.

As you pull me closer

There is a running rover

Baby it won't be over

Until you grip me through the shoulder

And keep the distance shorter

Because you're my ultimate comforter.

You are the reason my heart sings,

You are the reason my lips smile,

You are the reason my days are bright,

You are the only reason I live my life.

©Joyce.

30. Martha. KEMA.JUSU

SHE DESERVES BETTER

MARTHA JUSU IS A YOU GIRL FROM SIERRA LEONE ??, WHO IS INSPIRED TO DO THE WORK OF POETRY.

SHE STARTED SINCE 17YEARS OLD,ALTHOUGH SHE'S A SCIENCE STUDENT CAUSE HER DREAM IS TO SAVE LIFE BY BECOMING A NURSE. BUT SHE HAS A PASSION FOR POETRY. SHE DRINK INK AND EAT PAPER EVERY, WHAT AM SAY EVERY DAY SHE'S MOTIVATED TO WRITE POEM. HER POEMS ARE CREATIVE AND NOT PHOTOCOPIES. HOPE YOU

WILL LIKE HER WRITE UP

MY PEN, MY WEAPON.

My pen is my weapon,

With it, I'm a champion.

You are my solid sword,

I need no iron rod,

To build any tower,

You give me power.

In any battle, I count on you for victory.

You have stored it for me.

Many link soldiers, to conquer any failure.

Oh! My pen, my weapon.

When you're beside me I'm a winner.

Am free to be at any dinner.

In depression, you're my expression.

Now I understood the saying 'The Pen is Mightier than the sword ".

You are indeed a sword to me.

Oh! My pen is my weapon.

POETESS: MAT. D. POETESS✍?.

31. Jemima Wanjirú

Jemima is an 18 years old poetry lover and a poetess who is a Kenyan by nationality. She has co-authored 5 anthologies and awarded with onboard certificates and e-certificates. She began writing at her current age.

The Cold Sensation

I'm tired of yelling,

I'm tired of pretending,

Yes my river flows ,

My eyes ever full of salty waters,

Then down my backside,

It's out of pain.

Yes my pillow soaks my tears ,

I'm think of my five past years , then my next five years,

Have I ever will I ever sleep ,

They say time will tell,

Clock ticking slow,

I fear the known and unknown,

It's out of pain.

My life ever full of darkness,

I'm ever penniless,

The heads speak over me,

Nurturing ulcers allover ,

I don't afford a slice,

Yes I cry ,

It's out of pain.

My red liquor won't support ,

Violently they'll own my little,

Then my beak won't feed the beaks,

Because I sweat for them,

Yes it's a cold sensation,

Yes my life will be wet ever.

I will wait to rest ,

For I will pretend no more!

9 798887 491486

Printed by Libri Plureos GmbH in Hamburg, Germany